THE ESSENTIAL COLLECTION

VIVALDI

GOLD

Published by:
Chester Music Limited,
8/9 Frith Street, London W1D 3JB, England.

Exclusive Distributors:
Music Sales Limited,
Distribution Centre, Newmarket Road, Bury St Edmunds, Suffolk IP33 3YB, England.
Music Sales Corporation,
257 Park Avenue South, New York, NY10010, United States of America.
Music Sales Pty Limited,
120 Rothschild Avenue, Rosebery, NSW 2018, Australia.

Order No. CH69234
ISBN 1-84449-778-X
This book © Copyright 2005 by Chester Music.

Compiled by Quentin Thomas.
Arranging and engraving supplied by Camden Music.

Printed in the United States of America
by Vicks Lithograph and Printing Corporation.

Your Guarantee of Quality:
As publishers, we strive to produce every book to the highest commercial standards.
The music has been freshly engraved and carefully designed to minimize
awkward page turns to make playing from it a real pleasure.
Particular care has been given to specifying acid-free, neutral-sized
paper made from pulps which have not been elemental chlorine bleached.
This pulp is from farmed sustainable forests and was produced
with special regard for the environment.
Throughout, the printing and binding have been planned to ensure a sturdy,
attractive publication which should give years of enjoyment.
If your copy fails to meet our high standards, please inform us and we will gladly replace it.

www.musicsales.com

CHESTER MUSIC
part of the Music Sales Group

London/New York/Paris/Sydney/Copenhagen/Berlin/Madrid/Tokyo

Concertos For Violin(s):
from 'L'Estro Armonico' Op.3

from 'La Stravaganza' Op.4

from Op.7, Book 2

from 'The Four Seasons' Op.8, Nos.1-4

Concertos For Other Instruments:

Sonatas:

Vocal Works:

Antonio Vivaldi

It is believed that Vivaldi was born in Venice on 4th March 1678, the same day that an earthquake shook the great water-city. His father was a violinist at Saint Mark's in Venice and taught Antonio the instrument before they toured the Venetian region together as a performing duo. It is irrefutable that Antonio had red hair and that he was ordained into the priesthood; the evidence is overwhelming given his fantastic nickname the 'Red Priest'. What is less certain, is why he left the priesthood – most facts point to him suffering from asthma or angina. Central to Vivaldi's existence was the 'Conservatorio dell' Ospedale della Pietà' in Venice, a musical conservatoire for poor, illegitimate or orphaned girls. Vivaldi spent three periods of his life at this school between 1703 and 1738: as maestro di violino (violin teacher), then maestro di concerti (concert director) and finally as maestro di cappella (musical director).

Smaller works such as the *trio sonatas* characterised his early output, with concertos emerging by 1711. A set of concerti for violin(s) entitled *'L'Estro Armonico' Op.3* circulated Amsterdam and northern Europe, followed by *'La Stravaganza' Op.4*, fuelling musicians' desires to visit this legendary violinist and refreshing composer in Venice, and to offer him commissions. *'The Four Seasons'* were written in 1725, followed by eight other concertos with the less catchy title *'Contest of Harmony and Invention'*.

With a reputation that started to spread rapidly with visiting nobility and reciprocated invitations, Vivaldi spent a good deal of time travelling, often trying to promote his stage-works in the major opera houses of what now comprises Italy, and abroad in Prague, Amsterdam and Vienna.

Vivaldi was a massively popular composer in his day who wrote for audiences, not academics, and brought brightness and contrast to the formal and structured. His real contribution to the world of composition lies in his boldness and originality as exemplified in the concerti. He established the structure of three movements, aesthetically paced by the fast–slow–fast format, that was to become the backbone of the emerging symphony. He also used ritornello form, a fabulous vehicle for performers to strut their stuff in an improvisatory manner, while ensuring the return of the main thematic material to give a sense of cohesion. Features of his style include vigorous rhythmic patterns, often with downbeats full of activity, such as in the *Lute Concerto*. His frequent use of sequence is legendary (where a musical passage or phrase receives immediate repetition at a higher or lower pitch) enabling the listener to follow those captivating tunes all the more enthusiastically. He was an adventurous orchestrator, sometimes using unusual combinations of instruments at his disposal. Some of the concertos are unusually programmatic, following a story or description, such as *'The Four Seasons'*, which was a rare treat in those days outside of dance music.

How one counts the actual number of concertos written by this prolific composer is a complex task. As with many composers of the Baroque era, material was frequently 'borrowed' or reworked. Thus a cello concerto has a dual life as a bassoon concerto, a movement here for guitar is exactly the same as the movement there for violin, and so on. So estimates vary, but Vivaldi certainly notched up a total of between 450–550 concerti alone! Around 350 are for solo instrument (over 230 of these for violin), about 40 double concertos, over 30 for multiple soloists and nearly 60 for a small group of soloists without orchestra.

Vivaldi was also an extremely deft violinist, indeed, people made musical pilgrimages in an attempt to receive violin tuition from the great man, and it is of no surprise to see the influence his violin writing had upon the composer circuit. Johann Sebastian Bach studied his works assiduously, transcribing five of the Op.3 concertos into keyboard works at a time when the Germans began to imitate the style. Fame in his lifetime even spread to countries such as France, which at the time was very internalised into its own national schemes. By contrast, and of course many years later, Stravinsky said Vivaldi had not written hundreds of concertos – just one, repeated hundreds of times!

Most of his sacred vocal works were written for occasions and the girls at the Pietà, and often exhibit the vigorous influences of the concertos. Of some 50 operas thought to have been written by the 'Red Priest', nearly 30 survive. The *Gloria* is an example of Vivaldi's ability to offer a sacred work as an entertainment, utilising the best talents the Pietà would have had on offer and keeping the work 25 minutes long rather than turning it into a Mass.

As with all fashion, style soon gets cast out of the market-place as soon as tastes change direction. Vivaldi, facing poverty, sold most of his manuscripts for a pittance in an attempt to migrate to Vienna with hopes of gaining employment in the court of Charles VI (a big fan), but King Charles died soon after his arrival. Vivaldi died soon after on 28th July 1741, and was given a pauper's funeral, within one mile of where Mozart was to be buried exactly 50 years later, and with the young Joseph Haydn (one of six choristers) singing in the Requiem Mass at the great cathedral, Saint Stephen's, Vienna.

Like most composers, Vivaldi's life, music, and legendary status remained dormant after his death and awaited rediscovery for some considerable time. But it was worth the wait, when, in the late 1930s the Italian composer Alfredo Casella came across an incomplete work entitled *Gloria* by Antonio Vivaldi whilst rummaging through the National Library in Turin. Both regrettably and fortunately, a recording of it was made. It was regrettable because the recording was absolutely dreadful – and tragic that this would be the *only* definitive recording of *any* work of Vivaldi's until 1953. Yet the venture was fortunate, in that just 50 years on, Vivaldi has been truly discovered, with every musician in existence cutting their teeth on a Vivaldi concerto at some point.

Quentin Thomas, January 2005

Concerto No.1 (3rd Movement)

(from 'L'Estro Armonico' Op.3)

Composed by Antonio Vivaldi

Arranged by Quentin Thomas

Concerto No.2 (1st Movement)

(from 'L'Estro Armonico' Op.3)

Composed by Antonio Vivaldi

Arranged by Jerry Lanning

Concerto No.2 (2nd Movement)

(from 'L'Estro Armonico' Op.3)

Composed by Antonio Vivaldi

Arranged by Jerry Lanning

Concerto No.5 (2nd Movement)

(from 'L'Estro Armonico' Op.3)

Composed by Antonio Vivaldi

Arranged by Quentin Thomas

Largo

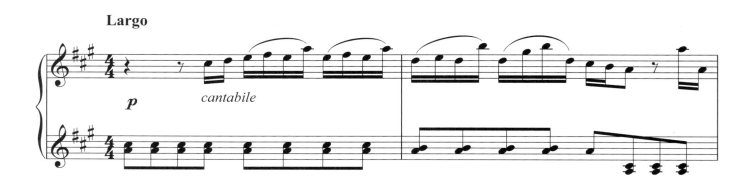

Concerto No.8 (1st Movement)

(from 'L'Estro Armonico' Op.3)

Composed by Antonio Vivaldi
Arranged by Jerry Lanning

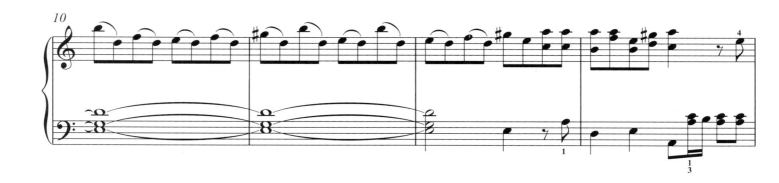

Concerto No.1 (1st Movement)

(from 'La Stravaganza' Op.4)

Composed by Antonio Vivaldi

Transcribed by Johann Sebastian Bach

Concerto No.6 (1st Movement)

(from 'La Stravaganza' Op.4)

Composed by Antonio Vivaldi

Transcribed by Johann Sebastian Bach

33

Concerto No.6 (3rd Movement)

(from 'La Stravaganza' Op.4)

Composed by Antonio Vivaldi

Transcribed by Johann Sebastian Bach

Giga
Presto

Violin Concerto No.2 (1st Movement)

(from Op.7, Book 2)

Composed by Antonio Vivaldi

Transcribed by Johann Sebastian Bach

Summer (2nd Movement)

(from 'The Four Seasons' Op.8, No.1-4)

Composed by Antonio Vivaldi

Arranged by Barry Todd

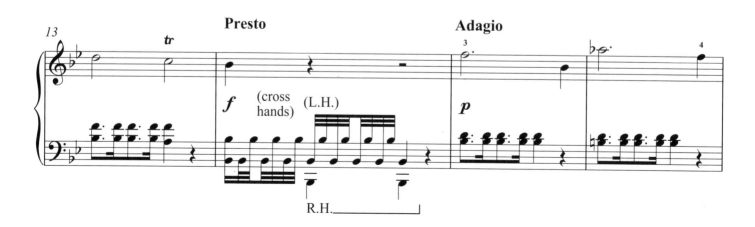

Autumn (1st Movement)

(from 'The Four Seasons' Op.8, No.1-4)

Composed by Antonio Vivaldi

Arranged by Barry Todd

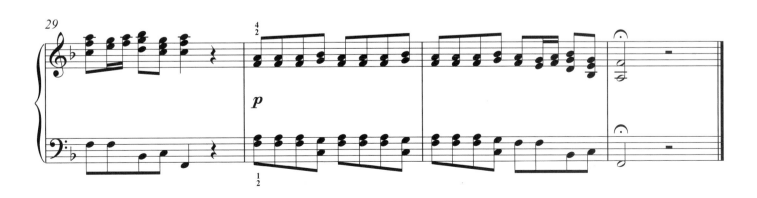

Autumn (3rd Movement)
(from 'The Four Seasons' Op.8, No.1-4)

Composed by Antonio Vivaldi
Arranged by Barry Todd

Winter (2nd Movement)

(from 'The Four Seasons' Op.8, No.1-4)

Composed by Antonio Vivaldi

Arranged by Barry Todd

Winter (3rd Movement)

(from 'The Four Seasons' Op.8, No.1-4)

Composed by Antonio Vivaldi

Arranged by Barry Todd

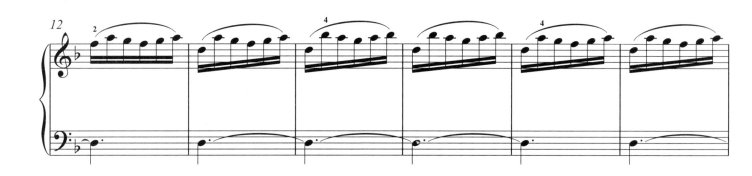

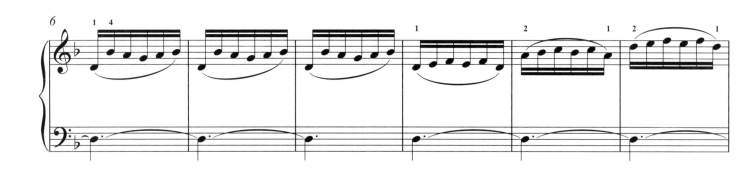

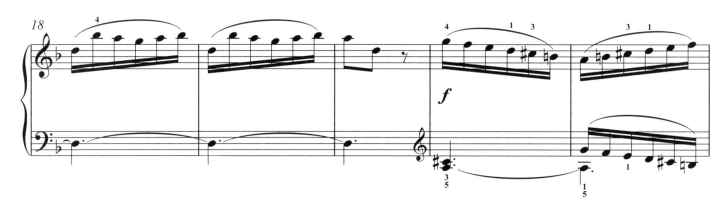

Spring (1st Movement)
(from 'The Four Seasons' Op.8, No.1-4)

Composed by Antonio Vivaldi

Arranged by Barry Todd

Spring (3rd Movement)
(from 'The Four Seasons' Op.8, No.1-4)

Composed by Antonio Vivaldi
Arranged by Barry Todd

Concerto for Two Violins, Lute and Continuo
(RV 93)

Composed by Antonio Vivaldi
Arranged by Quentin Thomas

I. Allegro giusto

II. Largo

p

With a little use of the sustaining pedal

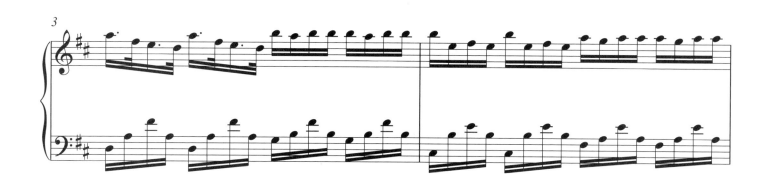

3

5

7

III. Allegro

Concerto for Two Mandolins, Strings and Organ, RV 532 (1st Movement)

Composed by Antonio Vivaldi

Arranged by Jerry Lanning

Concerto for Flute Op.10, No.2 'Night'
(5th Movement)

Composed by Antonio Vivaldi

Arranged by Jerry Lanning

Allegro

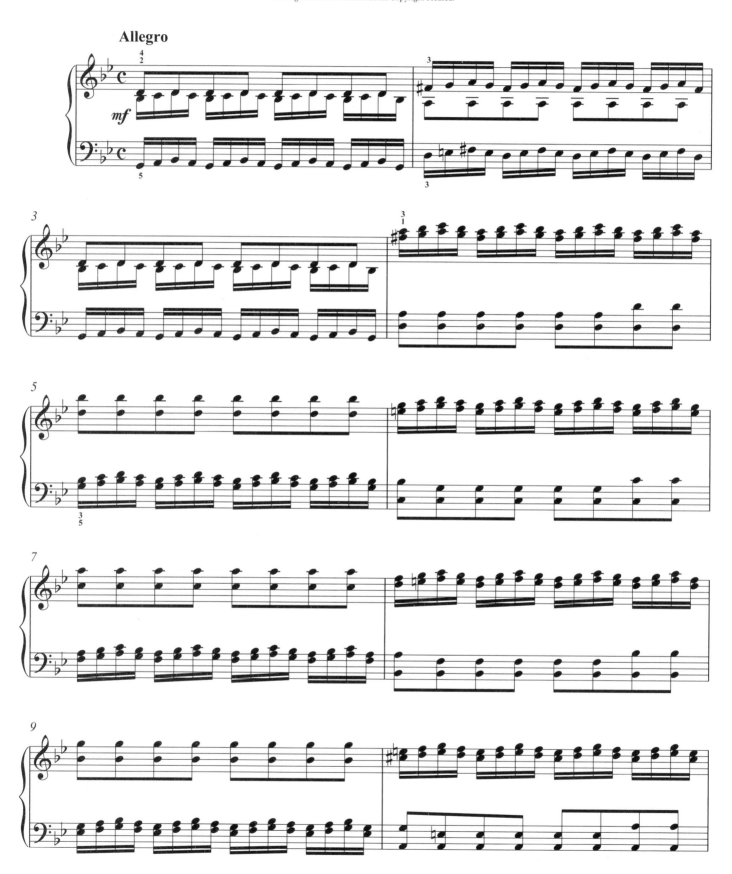

Concerto for Flute Op.10, No.3 'The Goldfinch'
(2nd Movement)

Composed by Antonio Vivaldi

Arranged by Quentin Thomas

'Un certo non so che'
(There's One, I Know Him Not)

(from 'Arsilda, Regina di Punto')

Composed by Antonio Vivaldi

Arranged by Quentin Thomas

'Beatus vir' / 'Potens in terra'

(from Beatus Vir)

Composed by Antonio Vivaldi

Arranged by Jerry Lanning

Allegro

'De torrente'

(from Dixit Dominus)

Composed by Antonio Vivaldi

Arranged by Quentin Thomas

'Gloria'

(from Gloria)

Composed by Antonio Vivaldi

Arranged by Quentin Thomas

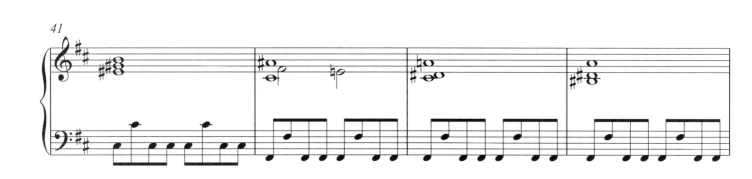

'Qui dat nivem sicut lanam'

(from Lauda Jerusalem)

Composed by Antonio Vivaldi

Arranged by Quentin Thomas

'Esurientes implevit'

(from Magnificat)

Composed by Antonio Vivaldi

Arranged by Jerry Lanning

Sonata No.1 for Cello and Piano
(4th Movement)

Composed by Antonio Vivaldi

Arranged by Quentin Thomas

Allegro

Trio Sonata Op.5, No.6 (1st Movement)

(for Two Violins and Continuo)

Composed by Antonio Vivaldi

Arranged by Jerry Lanning

Preludio

Largo

'Eja Mater'

(from Stabat Mater)

Composed by Antonio Vivaldi

Arranged by Jerry Lanning

'Stabat Mater dolorosa'

(from Stabat Mater)

Composed by Antonio Vivaldi

Arranged by Quentin Thomas

123456789